WE THE PEOPLE

Great Women of Pioneer America

by Sarah De Capua

Content Adviser: Jennifer Spencer,
Education and Collections Manager,
Sewall-Belmont House and Museum, Washington, D.C.

Reading Adviser: Rosemary G. Palmer, Ph.D.,
Department of Literacy, College of Education
Boise State University

COMPASS POINT BOOKS
MINNEAPOLIS, MINNESOTA

Compass Point Books
3109 West 50th Street, #115
Minneapolis, MN 55410

Visit Compass Point Books on the Internet at *www.compasspointbooks.com*
or e-mail your request to *custserv@compasspointbooks.com*

On the cover: Mother and children doing chores near their log cabin in the early 1800s

Photographs ©: North Wind Picture Archives, cover, 7, 17, 22; Prints Old and Rare, back cover (far left); Library of Congress, back cover; MPI/Getty Images, 5; Hulton Archive/Getty Images, 6; Peter Stackpole/Time Life Pictures/Getty Images, 8; Courtesy Scotts Bluff National Monument, 10, 21; Connie Ricca/Corbis, 12; Courtesy of Laura Ingalls Wilder Home Association Mansfield, Mo., 14; The Granger Collection, New York, 16, 25, 34; Photo Courtesy of the South Dakota State Historical Society-State Archives, 18; Corbis, 19, 38; University of Michigan Medical School Photographs, BL002009, Bentley Historical Library, University of Michigan, 23; Oregon Historical Society, #OrHi 4062, 24; Nebraska State Historical Society Photograph Collections, 27, 28, 29; The Denver Public Library, Western History Collection, Z-8811, 30; The Denver Public Library, Western History Collection, Duhem Bros. Album, X18554, 32; Denver Public Library, Western History Collection, Wm. Henry Jackson, WHJ-10632, 33; Architect of the Capitol, 36; Courtesy of The Bancroft Library, University of California Berkeley, 37; Oregon Historical Society, #OrHi 23881, 40; Oregon Historical Society, #4603, 41.

Managing Editor: Catherine Neitge
Designer/Page Production: Bradfordesign, Inc./Les Tranby
Photo Researcher: Marcie C. Spence
Cartographer: XNR Productions, Inc.
Educational Consultant: Diane Smolinski
Library Consultant: Kathleen Baxter

Creative Director: Keith Griffin
Editorial Director: Carol Jones

For Rebecca, a future great woman of 21st-century America. SDC

Library of Congress Cataloging-in-Publication Data
De Capua, Sarah.
  Great women of pioneer America / by Sarah De Capua.
    p. cm.—(We the people)
  Includes bibliographical references and index.
  ISBN 0-7565-1269-7 (hardcover)
  1. Women pioneers—West (U.S.)—History—19th century—Juvenile literature. 2. Women pioneers—West (U.S.)—Biography—Juvenile literature. 3. Pioneers—West (U.S.)—History—19th century—Juvenile literature. 4. Frontier and pioneer life—West (U.S.)—Juvenile literature. 5.—Social life and customs—19th century—Juvenile literature. I. Title. II. Series: We the people (Series) (Compass Point Books)
  F596.D357 2006
  978'.02'082--dc22   2005002472

TABLE OF CONTENTS

CHANGING THE COURSE OF HISTORY

What pictures come to mind when thinking of the American frontier? Cowboys and Indians? Gold and silver miners? Sheriffs, soldiers, and outlaws? What about pioneer women who traveled to the West in search of freedom, land, and opportunity? These women endured hardships, overcame challenges, and influenced American society in extraordinary ways.

They were businesswomen, miners, outlaws, artists, doctors, writers, sculptors, and actresses. They were wives of military men and explorers. They were lawyers and politicians. In most cases, their names are not well known, but they made their mark on society. They settled a land that was unknown to most Americans. While some became famous, the experiences of all these pioneer women helped to change the course of American history. Here are some of their stories.

A pioneer family headed west to Nebraska with their belongings in a covered wagon.

TRAILBLAZERS

Many pioneers were women who left fancy homes in the eastern United States. They traded houses with wallpaper, bathtubs, and gaslights for covered wagons and homes made of sod or logs. They tolerated the constant dust and dirt of the trail and the homestead. It was nearly impossible to keep things clean. Women exchanged their fashionable clothing for more practical high-topped shoes that protected their feet and sunbonnets that shielded their eyes from the bright sun. They had little privacy on the trail, and bathed in streams or water holes. They faced heat, droughts, tornadoes, and blizzards.

Women and children pose outside their log cabin in the West.

Women and children had many household duties.

Frontier homes were lit by candles, water had to be carried in a bucket from a well or stream, and food was cooked over a fire. Women such as Narcissa Whitman and Caroline Quiner Ingalls sacrificed much, but blazed a trail for others to follow. They made it possible for the women who came after them to build lives of excitement, adventure, and opportunity.

NARCISSA WHITMAN

Narcissa Prentiss lived in New York and dreamed of going west as a missionary. But her church would not allow single women to travel west. In 1835, she met Marcus Whitman, a missionary and doctor, and after knowing each other for a few days, they agreed to marry.

Whitman had been to Oregon and had returned east to find people to work with him there.

Narcissa Whitman (1808–1847)

Right after their wedding on February 18, 1836, they left for the Pacific Northwest with another missionary couple, Henry and Eliza Spalding, and a prospective missionary, W. H. Gray. It was a long and difficult journey. The women traveled by covered wagon, boat, and—most difficult of all—horseback, by riding sidesaddle. Narcissa and Eliza were the first white women some Native Americans had ever seen. They were the first white women to travel across the continent, and their covered wagon was the first to travel west over the Rocky Mountains.

The Whitmans established a mission at a Cayuse Indian settlement near present-day Walla Walla, Washington. In 1837, Narcissa gave birth to a daughter, Alice Clarissa, who was the first white baby born west of the Rockies. The day after her birth, curious Cayuse Indians gathered around to see her. In June 1839, Alice accidentally drowned. In the years that followed, the Whitmans took in several white and Cayuse children. They also helped pioneers as they arrived in Oregon. Their mission was an important stop along the Oregon Trail.

Life among the Cayuse was challenging for the Whitmans. The tribe was not interested in learning about Christianity. They did not need the white man's

Pioneers traveling west on the Oregon Trail often stopped at the Whitman Mission.

schooling. Likewise, the Whitmans did not understand the Cayuse lifestyle and traditions, although they tried.

Other problems arose with the large number of white settlers coming from the East. One group unknowingly brought a measles epidemic with them. Without natural immunity, half the local Cayuse died, including most of the children. The Whitmans survived.

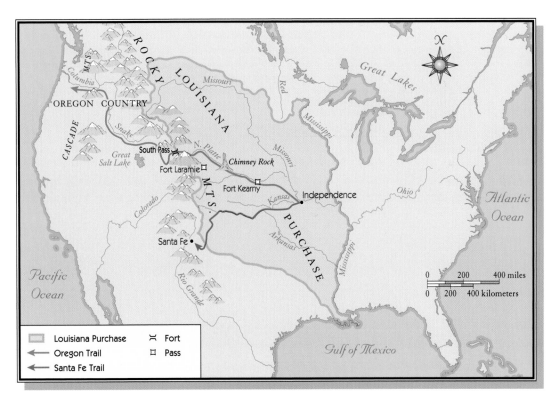

Travelers started their journeys west in Independence, Missouri.

11

On November 29, 1847, the Cayuse took their revenge. They killed the Whitmans and 12 others, and took 60 hostages, many of whom were later released. Narcissa was the only woman killed.

Wagon tracks of the Oregon Trail pass by the Whitman Mission National Historic Site.

Today, a 27-foot (8-meter) monument stands on a hill overlooking the Whitmans' mission settlement. It reads, "In patience, courage, and endurance, women proved man's equal."

The hill is called Shaft Hill. It was the Whitman family's favorite picnic spot. It was also the place where Narcissa taught her children about different kinds of plants and wildflowers. There, too, Narcissa watched for her husband to return from his work with other tribes.

Each year, thousands of visitors climb the hill to see the monument, which overlooks the Whitman massacre site. It honors Marcus Whitman and his wife, Narcissa Prentiss Whitman, the first missionary woman to live in the Pacific Northwest.

CAROLINE QUINER INGALLS

On December 12, 1839, Caroline Lake Quiner was born in Milwaukee County, Wisconsin. The first settler to the area had built a cabin there only three years earlier. Caroline

Charles Ingalls (1836–1902) and Caroline Quiner (1839–1924) were married for 42 years.

was the fifth of seven children born to Charlotte and Henry Quiner, who were farmers. From a young age, Caroline learned to help out at home. She fed chickens, churned butter, sewed, and cared for her younger sister and brother.

When Caroline was 5 years old, her father died. Five years later, her mother remarried. Caroline continued to help at home, but her education was important. School was in session only when there were enough children to attend, but Caroline was very smart and learned quickly.

It was during these school years that she wrote an essay about what "home" meant to her. She wrote, "How sweet … is the name of home! What music in that … sound!" Though Caroline's teacher told her she had a talent for writing, she was much too busy with the chores of daily living to write often.

Caroline Quiner married Charles Ingalls on February 1, 1860. Their life became a series of many journeys throughout the Midwest to small sod or log homes they built themselves. Each time they moved, the Ingalls family traveled in a covered wagon pulled by a pair of oxen or horses. They traveled all day and camped under the stars at night.

Meanwhile, the family grew. First, Mary was born. Then came Laura, Carrie, Charles—who died when he was 9 months old—and Grace. Whenever possible, the girls went to school. When they lived in a place without a school, Caroline taught them at home.

16

Carrie (from left), Mary, and Laura Ingalls

Travelers faced fierce blizzards and blinding snowstorms on the western plains.

The Ingalls family faced locusts and hailstorms that destroyed crops, and blinding snowstorms that lasted for days. During the hard winter of 1880–1881 in present-day South Dakota, the train carrying food and supplies could not reach their town for nearly eight months. Blizzard after blizzard howled through the area from October until the middle of April. The Ingalls family and many of their neighbors nearly starved to death. Through all these challenges, Caroline's ingenuity, like that of most pioneer women, solved many problems.

Caroline Quiner Ingalls died in 1924. She did not live to see the fame her daughter, Laura Ingalls Wilder, would achieve. Caroline's writing talent, courage, and determination were passed on to Laura, who created the *Little House* series of books. Written in

Laura Ingalls Wilder

the 1930s and 1940s, the books are a history of the growth of the Midwest from 1870 to 1890. They are among the best-loved children's books in the world and some of the most famous accounts of American pioneer life.

18

DOCTORS

At the beginning of the 1800s, the United States had no medical schools. Any man could practice medicine, but women could only be home nurses or midwives. By the mid-1800s, many medical schools for men had been established. The first medical school for women, the Woman's

Graduation ceremonies at the Woman's Medical College of Pennsylvania

19

Medical College of Pennsylvania, was founded in 1850, and a few others followed. Black women were not allowed to enter medical school. Still, they found other ways to learn about medicine and healing so they could care for the people in their communities.

Many people were shocked by women's desire to be doctors, but that didn't discourage these women. They worked hard in medical school. They studied long hours and passed tests, even though their male classmates made fun of them. They stayed focused on their goal of following in the footsteps of Elizabeth Blackwell, the first woman doctor in the United States, who graduated from medical school in 1849. Bethenia Owens-Adair and Susan LaFlesche Picotte were two such pioneer doctors.

BETHENIA OWENS-ADAIR

Bethenia Owens-Adair was born in Missouri in 1840. When she was 3 years old, her family joined a wagon train to Oregon. She did not like doing housework, the traditional chores for girls. Instead, she preferred chores that took her outdoors.

Nearly 400,000 people headed west on the Oregon Trail.

A nurse wears the familiar red cross.

Bethenia learned nursing and healing from her mother, Sarah Owens. Sarah became well known during the family's journey to Oregon. She nursed many sick and injured pioneers. Sarah knew how to make medicines from herbs. She believed good health came from exercise, healthy food, and plenty of rest. She passed on this knowledge to Bethenia.

Bethenia married at age 14 and became a mother at age 15. At age 18, she was divorced, which was not common at that time. Determined to make a good life for herself and her son, she took on nursing jobs. Doctors often asked her to help them treat patients. Women brought their sick babies and children to her. Eventually, Bethenia decided to become a doctor.

Students work in a lab at the University of Michigan Medical School in the late 1800s.

The few medical schools that existed in the West did not accept women. So in 1870, she entered the Eclectic School of Medicine in Philadelphia, Pennsylvania. She went on to the University of Michigan Medical School, one of the first medical schools in the country to educate both men and women. After graduation, she returned home to Oregon and opened her own practice in Portland. She was the first woman doctor in the Pacific Northwest. People there called her the "lady doctor."

Bethenia Owens-Adair (1840–1926)

At a time when women were not expected to pursue careers, Bethenia was determined to have one. Though she struggled with those who believed that, as a woman, she would not succeed as a doctor, she said, "I have never flinched from any undertaking, and I hope I never shall!"

For many of the years Bethenia practiced medicine, she lived with her second husband, John Adair, and their family on a farm. She sometimes rode her horse 30 miles (48 kilometers) to see patients. By the time she died in 1926, she had achieved great fame and respect as a doctor from women and men alike.

24

SUSAN LAFLESCHE PICOTTE

Susan LaFlesche, a member of the Omaha tribe of Native Americans, was born on the Omaha reservation in Nebraska in 1865. From the time she was young, she wanted to study medicine and care for her people. In 1884, she went to the Hampton Institute of Virginia, a

Susan LaFlesche Picotte (1865–1915)

school for freed slaves and Native Americans. When she graduated, she entered the Woman's Medical College of Pennsylvania.

In medical school, Susan studied difficult subjects. Her training included cutting open dead bodies to learn about organs, arteries, veins, and nerves. In letters to her family in Nebraska, she referred to herself as "Doctor Sue."

After three years at the Woman's Medical College, Susan returned to Nebraska as the first Native American woman doctor. She had graduated first in her class, but the U.S. government agent in charge of the Omaha reservation refused to hire her as the reservation doctor. Instead, she doctored children at the reservation school. Doctor Sue talked to their parents about cleanliness, healthy food, and ways to keep germs from spreading. She convinced the U.S. government to send more money for medicine and dental care.

After a few years, Susan was hired as the reservation doctor. She traveled long distances on horseback or by buggy to see patients. There were few nurses and no nearby hospitals, so she often lived with her patients until they felt better.

Susan LaFlesche Picotte (second row, wearing hat) with members of the Omaha tribe

Susan and Henry Picotte with their two sons, Caryl and Pierre

Susan married Henry Picotte when she was 29, and they had two sons. She continued to travel around the reservation treating patients, and many tribe members began to look to her as a leader. She took on that role and traveled to Washington, D.C., to try to convince the U.S. government to take better care of the Omaha. She was most dedicated, though, to the medical care of her people. She personally helped raise money to build a

hospital in the town of Walthill. The hospital was the first to treat whites and Omaha side by side. It was later named in her honor.

Dr. Susan LaFlesche Picotte suffered from a bone disease that caused severe ear pain. In 1915, she had surgery in an attempt to

Susan LaFlesche Picotte

correct the condition and died a few months later. She was 50 years old. She is remembered as the first Native American woman doctor in the United States and as the only person to treat every Omaha on her reservation at least once.

29

Social Reformers

They could not vote, own property, or make decisions for their children. They had to help their husbands repay debts. In pioneer America, women had few rights. They were not considered citizens until 1868, when the 14th Amendment

Men and women go to the polls in Colorado about 100 years ago. Most U.S. women did not get the right to vote until 1920 when the 19th Amendment was passed.

was added to the Constitution. The amendment reads in part, "All persons born or naturalized in the United States … are citizens of the United States and of the state wherein they reside."

This amendment was passed to make former slaves citizens of the United States. It only accidentally made women citizens, too. Nevertheless, women worked to gain full advantage of the new law. They wanted more rights, especially women's suffrage, which is the right to vote.

Two exceptional women helped change American society: Esther Morris and Abigail Scott Duniway.

ESTHER MORRIS

Esther Morris single-handedly brought women's suffrage to Wyoming, a rough and rowdy territory that was the first in the United States to allow women to vote.

Esther was born in New York in 1814. She became aware of the lack of rights for women shortly after her first marriage in 1841. When her husband died unexpectedly, she found she had no rights to his property or to their young son.

Esther Morris (1814-1902)

A wagon train moves west through South Pass, Wyoming, on the Oregon Trail.

In 1845, Esther married John Morris. After the Civil War ended in 1865, they moved with their three sons to South Pass, Wyoming, to mine for gold. After her marriage, Esther began working in the abolitionist movement and had a growing interest in the fight for women's rights. Once she had settled in Wyoming, she worked tirelessly for women's suffrage. She held tea parties for men running for local and territorial office. There she talked to them about why they should grant women the right to vote.

Women go to the polls in Wyoming, the first territory that allowed women to vote.

She supported William H. Bright, who was running for the Wyoming legislature. Bright believed since former slaves had the right to vote, women should, too. Esther encouraged others to vote for Bright, and he won the election. Soon after, Bright introduced a bill to the legislature. When the bill passed in 1869, women had the right to vote in Wyoming. They also had the right to own property, serve on juries, earn and keep money, and be the guardians of their children.

In 1870, in South Pass, Esther was appointed the world's first female justice of the peace. Newspaper reporters throughout the country made fun of her, but she did her job well, deciding 70 cases.

In 1892, Esther was given the honor of representing Wyoming at the Republican National Convention in Ohio. She officially cast Wyoming's votes for Benjamin Harrison, who went on to win the presidency. When she died in 1902, her son said, "The work she did for the elevation of womankind will be told in the years to come."

*A statue of Esther Morris represents
Wyoming in the U.S. Capitol.*

Today, a 9-foot (3-meter) bronze statue of Esther Morris stands in the U.S. Capitol in Washington, D.C. It bears the words, "Mother of Equal Rights." Her tiny log cabin home in South Pass, Wyoming, where she hosted tea parties and later held court, has been restored, and a plaque there marks her accomplishments.

ABIGAIL SCOTT DUNIWAY

Abigail Scott was born in Illinois on October 22, 1834, the oldest of 10 children. In 1852, her father decided to move the family to Oregon. The trip from Illinois by wagon train was long and difficult. Along the way, Abigail's mother and youngest brother died and were buried on the trail.

Deaths were common on the Oregon Trail.

Abigail Scott Duniway (1834-1915)

In Oregon, Abigail married Benjamin Duniway. Like others, they were farmers. Abigail also cooked, cleaned, washed clothes, fed chickens, and raised the couple's children.

All the while, she longed to do something more.

In 1859, Abigail wrote the first novel published in Oregon. It was called *Captain Gray's Company, or Crossing the Plains and Living in Oregon.* The book did not receive good reviews and was considered a failure.

38

After Benjamin was injured in a farming accident, Abigail opened a hat-making shop to help support her family. There she often heard women customers' stories of unfair treatment from their husbands and from laws that did not protect them. One woman's husband left town with all their money and belongings. Another woman's husband died, but the court would not allow her to have his money to support their children. Abigail was troubled by these stories, but she was unsure how to make women's lives better.

Benjamin told Abigail that things would not get better for women until they were allowed to vote. Abigail decided to devote her life to the cause. When the family moved to Portland, Oregon, she founded *The New Northwest,* a newspaper for women. She wrote articles in support of women's suffrage. Abigail invited two famous suffragists, Susan B. Anthony and Elizabeth Cady Stanton, to speak in Portland. Afterward, Abigail and Susan B. Anthony toured Oregon speaking out for women's suffrage.

39

WOMEN PAY TAXES!!
WOMEN OBEY THE LAWS!

Women and Children suffer from dirty streets, impure milk, adulterated food, bad sanitary conditions, smoke laden air, underpaid labor.

WOMEN CLEAN THE HOMES:
LET THEM HELP CLEAN THE CITY

| VOTE | 300 X 'YES' | AMENDMENT NO. 1, NOV. 5, 1912 |

It will give the women A SQUARE DEAL.
It will give your girl the same chance as your boy.

VOTES FOR WOMEN
COLLEGE EQUAL SUFFRAGE LEAGUE, 406 SELLING BLDG.

Oregon women received the right to vote in 1912.

In 1872, Abigail introduced a suffrage bill to the Washington territorial legislature, but it did not pass. She kept trying until 1883, when the bill finally passed. Next, Abigail worked for suffrage in Oregon, where she reminded people, "Even the mentally ill and criminals can vote." Only women could not. But the bill did not pass.

Abigail continued her work. She founded women's clubs, led parades, and spoke at rallies. By the time Oregon gave women the right to vote in 1912, the territory had become a state. At the next election, Abigail Scott Duniway became the first woman in Oregon to vote.

Abigail Scott Duniway was 80 years old when she died in 1915. She changed Oregon society forever and helped to bring about changes across the United States. She is remembered as one of the nation's leading suffragists.

These pioneer women, and others, are not just remembered for their accomplishments. Their more important qualities—courage, determination, and faith in their abilities—are part of our national heritage.

In 1912, Abigail Scott Duniway was the first Oregon woman to register to vote.

GLOSSARY

abolitionist—someone who supported the banning of slavery

gaslights—lights powered by burning gas; they worked better than candles and were used before the invention of the lightbulb

immunity—the ability of the body to resist a disease

justice of the peace—someone who hears cases in local courts of law

locust—a type of grasshopper that flies in huge swarms and eats and destroys crops

midwives—people, usually women, who assist women in childbirth

missionary—someone who travels to a new land to spread his or her religion

naturalized—made a citizen of a country after being born in another country

reservation—large area of land set aside for Native Americans

sidesaddle—uncomfortable riding position with both legs on the same side of the horse; the saddle itself

suffragists—women who worked for women's right to vote

DID YOU KNOW?

- In 1850, the U.S. government passed the Oregon Land Donation Act. This law gave 320 acres (130 hectares) of land to every settler and the same amount to his wife, although husbands were in charge of the land. This is the law that started the great movement of people from the eastern states to Oregon.

- Women and children crossing the Plains during the 1800s collected buffalo chips, or manure. It was used as fuel for campfires, and its smoke chased away mosquitoes.

- Known as prairie schooners, the wagons that most pioneers traveled in were about 10 feet (3 m) long, 4 feet (1 m) wide, and 2 feet (0.5 m) deep. A canvas cover stretched over bows high enough to allow a person to stand up inside the wagon. Sometimes pockets were sewn on the inside of the canvas to hold books, kitchen utensils, or fragile objects. The canvas-covered wagons reminded some of the white-sailed schooners that sailed the oceans.

IMPORTANT DATES

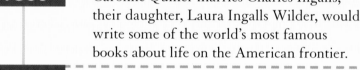

Timeline

1836 Narcissa Whitman and Eliza Spalding become the first white women to cross the continent and the first to live in the Pacific Northwest.

1860 Caroline Quiner marries Charles Ingalls; their daughter, Laura Ingalls Wilder, would write some of the world's most famous books about life on the American frontier.

1869 Wyoming grants women the right to vote.

1870 Esther Morris becomes the world's first woman justice of the peace.

1883 Washington Territory grants women the right to vote.

1912 Oregon grants women the right to vote.

IMPORTANT PEOPLE

BRIDGET "BIDDY" MASON (1818–1891)
Slave who was freed by a California court; she became a landowner and one of the wealthiest women in Los Angeles

GEORGIA ARBUCKLE FIX (1852–1918)
The first woman doctor in Nebraska, she founded a hospital in Gering, and practiced medicine until her retirement in 1916

MOLLY GOODNIGHT (1839–1926)
Texas ranch woman who helped to save the buffalo from extinction and encouraged her husband Charles' invention of a more comfortable sidesaddle

SUSAN SHELBY MAGOFFIN (1827–1855)
Pioneer who kept a detailed diary of her experiences as she traveled by covered wagon along the 1,000-mile (1,600 km) Santa Fe Trail in June 1846; her account is read by thousands every year and is considered a unique document of prairie life and pioneer spirit

PRETTY SHIELD (1850–1930)
Crow Indian healing woman who overcame her shyness to teach historians about her people so the Crow people and their traditions would not be forgotten

WANT TO KNOW MORE?

At the Library

Erickson, Paul. *Daily Life in a Covered Wagon.* New York: Puffin Books, 1997.

Katz, William Loren. *Black Women of the Old West.* New York: Atheneum, 1995.

Ketchum, Liza. *Into a New Country: Eight Remarkable Women of the West.*
New York: Little, Brown and Company, 2000.

Wilder, Laura Ingalls. Complete set of *Little House* books: *Little House in the Big Woods, Little House on the Prairie, Farmer Boy, On the Banks of Plum Creek, By the Shores of Silver Lake, The Long Winter, Little Town on the Prairie, These Happy Golden Years, The First Four Years.* New York: Harper Trophy, 1994.

On the Web

For more information on the *Great Women of Pioneer America*
use FactHound to track down Web sites related to this book.

1. Go to *www.facthound.com*

2. Type in a search word related to this book
   or this book ID: 0756512697

3. Click on the *Fetch It* button.

Your trusty FactHound will fetch the best Web sites for you!

On the Road

**Whitman Mission National
Historic Site**
328 Whitman Mission Road
Walla Walla, WA 99362
509/522-6357
To visit the site of the Whitmans'
home, learn about Cayuse culture,
and climb Shaft Hill to see the
monument erected there

Pioneer Woman Museum
701 Monument
Ponca City, OK 74604
508/765-6108
To see exhibits and artifacts
honoring pioneer women

Look for more We the People books about this era:

The Alamo

The Arapaho and Their History

The Battle of the Little Bighorn

The Buffalo Soldiers

The California Gold Rush

The Cherokee and Their History

The Chumash and Their History

The Creek and Their History

The Erie Canal

Great Women of the Old West

The Iroquois and Their History

The Lewis and Clark Expedition

The Louisiana Purchase

The Mexican War

The Ojibwe and Their History

The Oregon Trail

The Pony Express

The Powhatan and Their History

The Pueblo and Their History

The Santa Fe Trail

The Sioux and Their History

The Trail of Tears

The Transcontinental Railroad

The Wampanoag and Their History

The War of 1812

A complete list of We the People titles is available on our Web site:
www.compasspointbooks.com

INDEX

About the Author

Sarah De Capua is the author of many books, including nonfiction, biographies, geography, and historical titles. While researching this book, she enjoyed traveling to pioneer sites near her home in Colorado and learning more about the contributions of women pioneers to the settlement of the West.